un-coded woman

Anne-Marie Oomen

MILKWEED EDITIONS

The characters and events in this book are fictitious. Any similarity to real persons, living or dead, is coincidental and not intended by the author.

Published 2006 by Milkweed Editions
Printed in Canada
Cover design by Percolator
Cover photo by Samantha Grandy/iStockphoto
Author photo by S. Theo Early
Interior design by Percolator
The text of this book is set in Miller.
06 07 08 09 10   5 4 3 2 1
First Edition

Special underwriting for this book was contributed by Joanne and Phil Von Blon.

Milkweed Editions, a nonprofit publisher, gratefully acknowledges support from Anonymous; Emilie and Henry Buchwald; Bush Foundation; Patrick and Aimee Butler Family Foundation; Cargill Value Investment; Timothy and Tara Clark Family Charitable Fund; Dougherty Family Foundation; Ecolab Foundation; General Mills Foundation; Kathleen Jones; D. K. Light; McKnight Foundation; a grant from the Minnesota State Arts Board, through an appropriation by the Minnesota State Legislature, a grant from the National Endowment for the Arts, and private funders; Sheila C. Morgan; Laura Jane Musser Fund; an award from the National Endowment for the Arts, which believes that a great nation deserves great art; Navarre Corporation; Debbie Reynolds; Cynthia and Stephen Snyder; St. Paul Travelers Foundation; Ellen and Sheldon Sturgis; Surdna Foundation; Target Foundation; Gertrude Sexton Thompson Charitable Trust (George R. A. Johnson, Trustee); James R. Thorpe Foundation; Toro Foundation; Weyerhaeuser Family Foundation; and Xcel Energy Foundation.

Library of Congress Cataloging-in-Publication Data

Oomen, Anne-Marie.
Uncoded woman / Anne-Marie Oomen. — 1st ed.
        p. cm.
ISBN-13: 978-1-57131-425-3 (pbk. : acid-free paper)
ISBN-10: 1-57131-425-3 (pbk. : acid-free paper)
I. Title.
PS3615.57U53 2006
813'.6—dc22

                    2006020273

This book is dedicated to the women working third shift.

uncoded
woman

The titles of individual poems in this collection are drawn from the book *The International Code of Signals*, Pub. 102, Defense Mapping Agency Hydrographic/Topographic Center (Bethesda, Maryland, 1993). The signals are used by commercial and pleasure craft to communicate in situations where the safety of navigation or persons may be in jeopardy, particularly where there are language barriers. The code provides a simple method for communicating using pennants and flags and also includes telegraph and radio signals. The colors, shapes, and combinations of flags all contribute to the meaning of each individual message, which may be declarative statements, questions, or commands. For instance, sections of the *International Code* include such categories as division of time, latitude and longitude, and urgent and important messages.

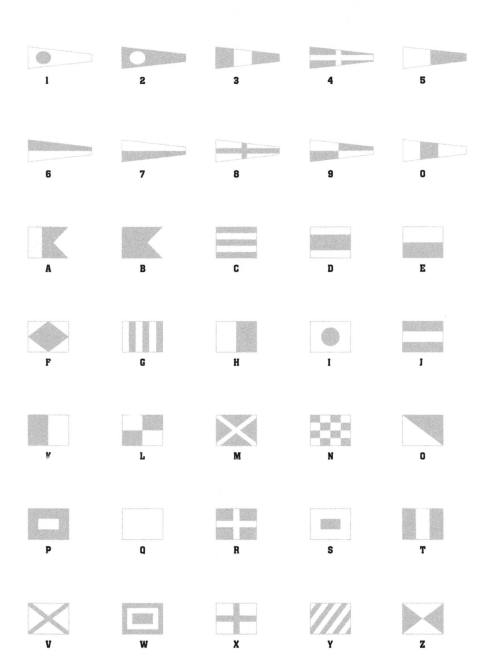

uncoded woman

I Have Taken the Line

How it all kicked off—I'm on the run.
This guy's hitching the I-55 on-ramp,
thumb like a scrap of flag.

His last name sounds Indian.
Bloodlines must be watered down—
looks German. First name's Barn.

My truck is military green and stole,
rest of me so black and blue, so down
and out, I don't know where I'll go.

He says, *Come up North with me.*
He says, *I know a old trailer*
where the river forks into the lake.

The cold will wake the dead,
but if the current's right, the fish
will bite. We can buy a line.

The murk of his hand-rolled smoke
is what I want first. Something certain
to wrap in. Something hot

and hurtful that I already know,
that once in a blue moon
still surprises me.

I drive like a flood busting open sluice
gates, like my whole past wants me
drowned but I'm not going down.

A body can do this once or twice a life—
just grab a line. And plain miss when
that cigarette butt turns to ash,

burns to something shaped
like a cement anchor bucket.
Pulls you under anyhow.

My Radio Direction Finder Is Inoperative

For a while, running away blooms yellow as cucumber
with that scent that cleans like rain,

but in the end all you're doing is getting lost
all over, and for all those miles and road meals,

it doesn't stop the wish like a hard kiss
to know why the screen door slammed,

why the bruise of Mama's hands never hurt me,
why the mast of Daddy's limbs always did,

or why I am named Beatrice.

It's like this: Just when I think memory is tucked
into some shotgun with the safety on,

that delicate odor of cucumber goes tacking
on the wind; then there's the forged kiss

of remembering, a cracked-ice click just
before all the guns go off at once.

For short, they call me Bead—
a thing so small it should be forgotten.

NE

You Should Proceed with Great Caution

Barn and me stand where the river
joins from two branches.
He tells me: *They smell it.*

They taste the water.
Only one branch is good for them fish.
Steelhead start up South Branch,

but you watch, they'll drift back.
He points to the dark bodies.
Taste ain't right, been spoiled.

Runs clear enough, but logging
washed the topsoil in, buried
the stony places, no shallow beds

for that female to slap her body down,
get them eggs out. They fall back,
swim around for while,

choose the North Branch.
Still got a few clean pools,
plenty big rocks.

Fish can tell pretty quick.
He keeps talking. I'm tasting currents,
grit of one, thick of another,

smelling the differences
between rivers, trying to scent
where home is, if I want it.

All Lights Are Out Along This Coast

After charred burgers at Art's Bar,
     we drive across the narrows,
     two-track only wide as my bald tires
     divides two mud-bottomed lakes.

It's okay so long's he doesn't ask for my insides.
     And if the buckshot-pocked door
     of this old Airstream will just open,
     maybe the trip to the back bedroom

will offer some kind of shelter.
     The me that's a school of minnows will turn
     all together into the shallows, point
     toward some more restful shore.

But when he breaks the lock, the door shrills open,
     screams like gulls on trash.
     He elbows me up, shoves
     me down the hall, promises

Tomorrow we'll get lights turned on.
     But I know this routine,
     how there is no answer
     to dead air and musk-cupped sheets.

When morning drops in on this piece of crap,
     even those rifle holes
     will not give light—just
     black holes clotted with rust.

Still, he does what he says:
      squeezes pennies into a fuse box,
      runs an extension cord to the outhouse,
      flicks a switch and smiles like Jesus.

I Am Going Ahead

I wake to sour lake wind
and sparrows' requiem.

Chatter puts me in mind of statues
in a New Orleans cemetery

down where I come from—my
Daddy took me after Mama passed—

her and the other dead came too close,
and all those birds calling me out,

and tinny slivers of lacquer
peeling off the Virgin's eyes.

She would see the truth:
Here I am, all undressed,

no place to go.
No more jittery possibility.

It's a sticky kind of sick—
that I have landed where there's water,

muddy and familiar.
Light pumps against the cracked glass.

Dawn, this man calls it.
Surf drowns the sparrows' song—

if you can call their racket that.
I scrape paint off the blank-eyed walls,

catching chips like shards of bird bones
under my nails. The dead back off.

Towing Is Impossible under Present Weather Conditions

First off, lake here's too damned big.
I did not choose this *ocean*,
though this man would have me think so.

For him, we shape our lives like Anishinabe
shaped clay pots round as pears so they'd
stay put in the sand passes for soil here.

Me, I know what comes, comes. I duck
if I can, but I can't change what I know—
that lake is out for me.

And no matter how kind his voice
places words like berries on a plate
I can tell when I'm being suckered.

Barn tells me there are ways to take it,
ways a body can be *made clean* by
those waves big as horses' asses.

I know stupid when I see it.
I know drowning would be just
one more death by black water

like the one I'm hiding.
Come in? he asks, pulling on me.
I tell him, *You make me, I'll run.*

The waves are made by wind.
They do not choose the wind.
Life is one bad question with one bad answer.

I Have Sighted Survival Craft...

When he teaches me to swim these waves,
he warns about *undertows*. When top currents
roll in, underneath one sucks you out
like a mouth, a tongue to take you down.
Fucking deceptive, he says.

When it's too much for me, when I can't
slam the brakes on this brain full
of sand-blasted interrogatives,
I strip down to my own skin—
I want that undertow to yank me down.

It is there. I feel its question
taste my ankles, thighs;
feel the Braille of that fickle signal
named thrill,
and its partner, fear.

But it will not take me.
I have run the risks of drowning
so many times,
I have learned to swim sideways—
like a crab, right out of it.

Now I swim this water every day, risking
one cold current for the other—
learning how to be a swimmer
and how to fucking be—
the second is undertow to the first.

Up the coast a piece, a museum.
Old Lifesavers Station. I pull in, let the truck cool.
Walk around like old things interest me.

I stroke prows of boats once used to save
the drowning. Who the hell climbs whole out
of the lives they got in these swamps and lakes?

On the bookstore shelf, a paperback
flyspecked with constellations and alphabets
claims the flags—*pennants* they're called—

like the word *penance*—all have meanings
particular and on-file as my daddy's
thumbprints pressed on baby skin.

Each flag means a letter, two or more together,
whole new questions. Like *XQ*
What weather are you experiencing?

Let me tell you about weather:
Manitou wind they talk about up here
is just a colder killer than heat and hurricane,

or the tirade of a drunk gone sour in the gut,
reaching for a wrist not yet healed from the last twist.
That's weather. I steal the book.

Maybe the codes will teach me to cipher
distances, remember the secrets I hold
but don't care for light to shine on.

I'd like to see across that lake.
Learn how to say I'm sorry.
Book falls open.

Shows me how things might mean.
Forgiveness is not one of the letters.
But there are others that look like kin.

Alpha

The First Letter, Sometimes Used as Greeting

Cleaning suckers, his mama's hands
close around this spring-running fish,

sliver of river slapped on the gutting table.
She stills its sucking with a cleaver.

Fillet blade scatters scales like sticky coins.
It's a Menominee, she says.

She chops the fish in half and gasps—
she who has seen everything these rivers can puke,

even once the body of a great sturgeon—
as long as a human, with eyes full of God's ghosts,

frayed with weed and skin like silver gone to rot—
even that did not take her breath

as this does, this bone-lined hollow
spilling a thousand tiny suns from its tight pocket.

Jesus. Look, Honey. I watch her fingers squeeze
the roll of eggs into a yellow mound.

He don't use roe for bait. She drops them
into the bowl of my palms. No apology.

Small spheres cling to my fingers.
What does it mean that they

let that sturgeon's body float back out?
The first gesture water makes with cells

it also makes with death.

B

I Am Discharging Dangerous Goods

I toss the ruddy roe
into the weedy current—
nothing as gone
as the look of eggs
spreading like a sheer cloud
in river wash.

The fish eat the roe.

I know I am part of it,
but not the part I want to be.
Folks will never say,
but I am the second sound,
letter that comes after,
long-haired woman,

tosser of eggs,
charged with danger
and knowing—
a million tiny golden apples—
or stars—ticking their soft
if, if, if.

HM 1

Survivors Are in Bad Condition

We're slugging back his paycheck
in shots, looking at silence
like it was a lottery number gone bad.
In winter, a certain hunger burns

like old tires can't get put out,
smokes our faces until we're blind,
and just when I'm sure Barn will throw a bottle
just to start some other body swinging,

Charlene, the barber, comes cussing
through the weighted door,
hollering that *some you*
assholes better come help right now

or she'll give bad cuts to the first dozen dares
cross her shop threshold.
Men lean back their stools, look happy,
What'sa trouble?

Hit a buck down at the narrows,
not dead but can't get up, crying like a baby,
and my front end's busted.
Who's got a gun?

Two Copemish boys and Barn
move out, leaving me to think about roadkill.
Even with the poaching,
herd's too big, deer run like they meant to,

right in front of our trucks,
leaving our brains, if we got any left,
to remember other things
that come too quick out of the dark.

Or is it that we thrust
ourselves in front of light and speed,
chrome death grilling the dreams
of our ditch-ridden lives?

We stare up from dirt,
hearing the sound of loss
whir past, or the curse
of the one coming to finish us off.

HM 2

Survivors Are in Good Condition

After-hours, Jack swings by,
all smiles. Char grabs a six-pack,
promises good cuts all round.
He tows her home.

Barn traipses in the back door,
fresh haunch hanging off his shoulder,
chucks it on the cutting board
like it was dead meat. It is.

He and Carl pull out knives that have names,
ones they keep folded
in quiet pockets, ones they finger
if a man's look isn't what they like.

They slice it cross-grained, delicate
as whittlers. They slice it thin,
like was their mama's last pie.
Carl turns the flame back up.

They roll the meat in salt and white flour,
and when the grill is smoked
with onions, they toss the slivers on,
just a whisper of heat to sear in

that juice, seal what's left of the wild
from that impact and blast.
And then we're reaching, all of us
eager as starved dogs,

hungry for the roadkill of what we are,
all we have. Blood-tipped fingers
lift and taste, fed by meat
still shot through with running.

PG

I Do Not See Any Light

Ice is thick as concrete block, and the lake's surface
is so solid I think the past's gone still with it.

And here comes an Alberta Clipper, Alaskan heartbreak,
jet stream clotted with Arctic amnesia—

I could learn to live here.

Then the ice drill shows up in my own hands,
spirals down, chips a hole just big enough

to plunge a line all the way to rancid mud.
Why do I have to follow it down?

Under that ice, the only bite is memory: hot oil
spills down a cheek, hot blood

pools in the palm, skin blasted open
with—what was it—a pencil? It's the same as a blade.

All because I learned to read and Daddy did not.
Memory makes me laugh in the cold—that kind of fever.

Every day I ask the same question: How far to rock bottom,
how long before this lake will either freeze to the core

or let me drop this bait without bringing up the dead
caught in the hook of my own making?

Then I could stay.

Boats Cannot Be Used to Reach You

Ice is gone honeycomb bad. Kids on snowmobiles
stalled out. That's why it happened.
A body can get over weakness if you got some push.

At rest, it all gives way. No amount
of lifesaving or lifeboats or godforsaken
codes could pull them in.

The one went back for the others—he
got sucked down too. Helmets,
boots, the weight of panic did them in.

That harbor where it happened sticks in my craw
every time I look. Which is every day.
I come away dry eyed and weasel pissed.

The finches coming to the feeder
are quicker than those kids. If a branch gives
way birds just spread their wings,

That's what I wish for those boys.
Light bones. Wings. Momentum.
No use.

Weak ice—even I know you don't
stand still on weak ice. I tell myself,
keep moving. Fly.

I Am Having Engine Trouble but Am Continuing . . .

Pickup stalls on Snitch Road, engine dead.
My headlights can the night, sight
a critter climbing through osier.

She waddles the ditch,
slips into shallows. My beams toss back
her gloss, then just her wake.

One of the last in these parts.
Talk to me, I whisper.
I want to know:

> *Will you stop the creek,*
> *shape one of those wide ponds*
> *bordered with stump poplar?*
>
> *Will you burrow under, hollow*
> *out the mud? Build a fortress of*
> *the lost ifs and dead maybes.*

Geesh. Questions cheesy as old frosting.
Beaver's gone. Truck engine flares.
I backfire my way home.

Darkness just gets darker,
keeps its secret animal
invisible as the trouble some call love.

I Wish to Communicate with You

I shouldn't write again, Mama, you can't answer.
But I got to ask. You know March up North is dirty
as a swamp snake. That thin-skinned horizon
out on the lake splits open nothing

but the color of decay. We aren't sure of things—
not our quiet over coffee and toast,
not even when we feel the wind shift—
some mule kick gone out of it.

Did you ever feel, having been
betrayed so many times by so many men,
and by the jukebox song of your own
living, you could not trust your fingertips?

Mama, look back at my winter-tinned letters.
Tell me, was it still cold this time last spring?
Or is it colder now? Did we ever
walk out in honest air, warm, holding hands?

Where Are You Bound For?

The run commences and the steelhead lean into the flow
like life mattered. I don't get it,

how we just keep going,
mistaking it all until we're stuck

as those prehistoric monsters,
sinking in muck, and we don't know how

to decipher foot from mire
and meanness from its mirrors.

Barn stands in river cold so fierce
it could take his balls,

but he casts, over and over,
for the ones strong enough to be first.

The fish come on, doing what they do,
mistaking hook for good,

spear for green,
and net for weed.

Lives mired with betrayal—
like us, like them—the way they trust

rivers for their redds
but it binds them to their deaths

which is not a moment like some folks say,
but a place in the cold

that we are drawn to like a river,
fishing for a code.

PR 1

You Should Come as Near as Possible

With Barn, I watch a pair of steelhead
hold their place in the Platte,
her at the gravel bed, him gray

and hovering, warding off
foreign males, the marks
on his body possessive

as spilled ink. He bucks and snaps
at the others, and his sound,
if there were one, a growl at the moon.

And though Barn has watched
this coupling for decades, he
cannot tell me what happens next.

The male shimmies, draws
near her tail, slides over.
Side by side. Shadow. Shadow.

In the narrow current,
they swim together.
They shiver.

We can barely see it—the quiver
before he falls back, quick
arrow into the current below the rocks.

Then the radical gesture. She
flips to her side, slaps down her
silver body against hard stones.

Don't let the old-timers fool you.
It is not a beautiful sight,
except for the light from her belly,

gorged with river. From her liquid bones
she forces a thousand eggs into a tomorrow
where they will also tremble and slap.

They do this all the afternoon. I watch
like a sinner who loves her sin, a voyeur
of river with this man who tells me

without any shame,

There, there, she's doing it.
Woman, she's ready again.
Oh God, she'll fill the river.

JB

There Is Danger of Explosion

Then the season's gone to hell, snow turns
to a crust of waste, shore peppered
with zebra shells marked with lines of sin.

Barn's so picket faced, I know he's spoiling
for a fight. I been waiting for his brain to boil
down to dry. Show me what kind

of burned and mean he really is.
I get ready to fire up the truck and run.
But in a language he mostly does not know,

he sings songs without words,
walks the beach, stares hard at the scaffold
of a wreck. His voice heaves

through trees older than the gods who died.
Like that mythical bear, Mishimokwa,
the old teachers talk about, he is waiting.

Watching. After six days, the spill
of rocks on the south slope
looks like faces at peace again.

What happens to me then
is an answer from the stars.
No one sings when they're mad.

All Persons Lost

Overlooking cranberry bogs,
graves so old their stories fade
like stars in night haze.

One stone marks Elvira French, 1827–1907,
mistress, gossip claims,
to the one doctor in these parts.

Birthed three of his kids,
never married,
buried the babies with his name:

a girl, 1846, dead at six weeks,
boy two years later, dead at six weeks,
another boy in 1850.

I make out *Joseph* by tracing—
and *lost*—strange word for death,
as though the possibility existed

for being found—*lost*
at eleven months and six days.
Hard numbers.

Then the man's stone, Walker.
Ten feet away hers,
separate as stone piers.

Would he not claim you?
Or was it you, Elvira,
knowing this world is lawless

in the face of local shame,
begged a name for your kids
but refused one for yourself?

Kept your distance as code
for defiance? Your version
of a stolen pickup?

Damn straight. That's why
I traipse the ridge on my good days.
Any name he offers, I'll refuse too.

See how it is?
This rise was shoreline
ten thousand years ago.

Marks the high-water line,
sudden pitching drop-off point
under which the sour bushes grow like crazy.

Weather Is Good

Season turns into a party gone wild
the steelhead rush into by the hundreds,
bullying as they spawn.

They leap for the gravel redds,
smack the surface so hard
they wake us at night,

spelling out their lives in new letters.

It's loud as a full moon inside me.
When I look at the codes, it
seems they say, *You want it, take it.*

Even the dark outside the trailer's wreck
pulls the crocus up with its heat,
bright pennants that pass for things that last.

JO

I Am Afloat

Listen, flood comes on fast as fish strike
after a ten-hour rain, shatters the dam
at North Branch like it was made of sticks.

Midnight. The narrows' two-track
is a black water needle, then gone.
Swamp's a greasy rise against the stoop.

Barn throws switches,
pulls on waders, tells me,
tells *me* to crawl on his back.

I tell him he's nuts. Water seeps
over the linoleum like slime mold.
When we make it to the pickup,

starter's already soaked.
I know he can't carry me all that way.
Hell, there's not a way anymore.

He shucks off the waders,
ties the towrope round
my waist, ties it round his,

grins like a old man seen too much,
flips down his tailgate, sees my face
splashed with muck and terror, says,

Hey. Just walk by feel.
Walk by feel? Asshole.
He knows my story with water.

We make it out. At the township hall,
I pull blankets around my shoulders,
stare at all those careful-haired,

plump-as-ripe-apples, been-there-since-God
village women. Soup and baked beans
and twenty kinds of Jell-O,

and don't think I'm not grateful
but it's the Jell-O that sparks me,
after this diet of lard and scared,

all their little canned oranges
and marshmallows, their version
of comfort in the North.

Hey, I been in it up to my armpits,
river and trash thrashing around me
like an old message, finding my way

by feel. How did he know, with all his own
pasts and ghosts, that was the only way?
That's when I decide.

FO

I Will Keep Close to You

So. After I marry Barn, I watch him fish. Salmon,
trout, perch, bass run to his lines and nets.

I guess if they must be caught, it would best
be his wide hands, large as burdock leaves,

his touch
sweet as bait on skilled line—

and the kill, when the time comes,
small as a star.

I don't see all this right off,
how fish ponder the map of river veins

on the backs of his hands—
how they come rest in his palm.

I tell you, I want to keep close, to become
acquainted with currents quiet as backyard air,

to be as attentive as fish are
to the oldest bedding places. I want it

to be as though fish caught me,
nibbling my whole body, spreading out

like spokes, a veiled wheel of fish touch,
coupling me with water.

I would not even know they had taken me.
I do not know now,

traveling as I am into his liquid hours,
casting into his dorsal pools.

QX

I Request Permission to Anchor

The day they sink footings for our cabin,
I come adrift, starting one task, then another,
nothing holding me.

Standing at the ruined trailer, I smoke,
ask twice if I should stay
but what did I expect—there's no answer

to that kind of pariah question.
Then the semi, big cylinder stirring
its stew of stone growls into the woods.

I touch the trees nearest me, whisper
that this mess and noise are short-lived—
I can't help it: I come close

as I ever have to what my mama called prayer—
go figure. Me, the one who never asks,
I am asking to cast an anchor into dirt.

I Have a Pilot on Board

Charlene cuts hair in her made-over garage.
She went to beauty school for two weeks.
Rest is instinct.

She's bottle blond and scarlet nailed.
She is how lovely and used
a woman can get. She told

me about the library where
I go twice a week now,
just to cradle books and bring

home one or two to unfold
and hold and let them take me
to places so far away that I believe

in them. She won't cut it.
I tell her I'll do it myself.
Why, girl? It's your one

moment of luxury, that hair.
I tell her I need the money.
We been eating lake trout for weeks.

I want some pork fried deep
as they do in the South,
something that goes with Bays.

She combs and combs, asks slow-like,
What Barn's doin? I tell her
about the trouble with the nets.

She snorts, *Fishing rights?*
Well, he's in it up to his nuts,
that's for sure.

She says all the more reason
not to cut. She lifts a strand,
Sister, there are other ways

to get bacon on the table.
I been there, I tell her,
fighting to remember I am not there

anymore, that I don't need
to do anybody for money.
She laughs at my wrong head,

Not that, though that works
when it needs to. You're young,
but there's legal stuff. Try the grocery.

It turns me around then, my brain
hears the Old Man's voice,
scrape that shit, hang that carcass—

open your blouse and my gray buttons
flipping like coins through the air—
his fist brittle as frozen spittle.

Work was all about a brutal thing
that hit the skin, tore some flesh,
and left work still undone.

Work was never something I asked for,
not ever anything longer, worth more
than the length of my hair.

But here Charlene is telling me
they might need me down at Deerings,
that I could work for pay,

and not be hurt
by who asked me to do it.
She combs until it shines.

HY 4

What Is the Name of the Vessel with Which You Collided?

Fire. Village men call in the night—
even Barn—so desperate for help
they'd welcome half-breeds.
Abandoned boarding house.

Flames gunked with soot.
Air curled like singed hair.
Big Carl says *body count*.
Kids flopping.

Place had no doors, just "Keep outs."
Clear invite.
Cutter's boys, that mental
girl with the dreads—all too

unruly for foster care,
not yet bad enough for jail.
When it cools,
Barn sifts what's left for bones,

stays there nights, sings again.
I bring coffee, ask if he's taken
up the death medicine.
He frowns, shakes his head,

muttering about Indian bullshit
dancing in my head.
Where'd you get that?
Wouldn't you want to be found?

The ship of his eyes moves out
over bigger water than I can name.
Found? A word that strikes two ways—
bodies floating up through ash,

others floating down.
Empty vessels that catch you up
where you least expect—
and if you're smart,

are never given names.
I'm getting this:
Death is not good medicine
for the living.

RE

You Should Change Your Berth

I'm so scared I'm pissed, but I get that job.
Then the wasp of what I want
bumps the ceiling, yellow-winged tick
haunting the graveyard shift.

I shelve stock where it belongs,
mark the cost of everything like it counted.
Third night of that shit, stacking goods
people don't need onto racks that won't hold,

I walk out, drive to the ash heap
where Barn still sorts for teeth,
melted spoons, metallic rot of grief.
He will not leave those coals,

maybe his kin, maybe a song he hates
about the way they were left alone
in a place that wasn't safe.
I know. When he says no,

I hold his own rifle to his head,
push him in the truck, open his shirt,
lick the smoke off his skin,
take him in like I'm death medicine.

What does it mean to feel my hands
put a thing, *a man* in place,
for once forgetting my own wish
to burn or drown or be forgotten?

Raft Has Reached the Shore

There comes a day, warm as biscuits from the stove,
green shoots coming up through disturbed soil—
though they should know better. The cabin's done
enough for our winter-puckered lives so we move in

and there's some sunlight falling in the door.
Barn can work outside again, angle the chisel
into paired pine two by sixes, routing
grooves for a ladder to the loft.

First time since October last,
I scrub breakfast tins on the stoop,
rinse everything twice in lake water,
let them wind-dry, think the day is kind.

He shapes the grooves in which to slide
the treads that hold the stringers tight.
His tapping is a slow woodpecker,
chipping free the rotted grain.

Tonight we'll step up to the moon
to float on the inland sea we share again.

There Is Good Holding Ground in My Area

For a while, no dead fish
stinking up the shore
and sleep is a fine new weather.

On the high ground, he runs a fence
to keep out deer. I plant tomatoes, beans,
collard greens I crave,

and even though they freeze out, enough
will live to fill us until the cold comes on.
I'm learning, certain desires are like that.

Once, he walks out with a hoe
to help with the pigweed and knotgrass,
catches me with a fist of wet loam,

smiles a new star, wraps
his beefy hands around mine. I let him.
Maybe dirt moors us more than water.

I Cannot Save My Vessel

Shrub of purple lilac, heart-shaped leaves,
stone basement caved as an old face—
settler's homestead where the foxes hide
their den under what was a potato bin.

If I'm quiet, they let me creep through,
watch awhile. The kits like popcorn.
They toss it, tiny white birds
broken in their small teeth.

They could hear the lake all day.
They could drink from shallows,
chase minnows. The bitch brought
catch from the last of the run.

I was so sure they were a secret,
a thing I could hold
like only a few other things I hold,
a book of codes,

a past.
The pelts showed up
at Wild Market
three weeks after they disappeared.

Barn said some fool at Art's Bar
told him some other damn fool
had tamed them, they were
that easy to trap.

I heard once the old homestead wives
buried their stillborn babies
under lilac bushes. I want
to crawl into their den,

let it cave in,
let the white birds fly
up into the purple air
with all the secrets.

Light Has Been Extinguished

Today I got caught reading
at the checkout, customers
whining all down the filthy aisle,

spilling their so-called necessities:
tampons, six-packs, milk, chew.
The boss said not to come back.

Stock boy laughed,
skinny girl on checkout two
glanced at the title.

It was not a romance.

I come back to the dark place,
to the scrub acres where the cabin sits,
where these cloudy nights work on me.

You know, old-timers say it's best
to look at a sky without stars—
it will show you what you are

without any light at all.

UC

Is a Pilot Available in This Place?

Only one birch here not yet gone
to blight, dirty sleeve shines
its tattered column even in
this spring racked with fog.

Not yet riddled with punk, it holds
up a night sky that's too close,
holds up blind stars who see who I am,
not who I could be. I follow its rules:

Hide in the dark.
Stand alone.
Move when the wind does.
Don't talk.

Time cheeks my ankles, making them twitch.
Barn and me switch to salvage,
abandoned cottages on the North Branch.

He cops two double-hungs for our loft,
says we'll like the view, open water
right from our bed.

Rusty nails, warped boards. Decay.
Yet he can pull a window whole
from its sill of rot without breaking it.

Nails squeal loose from laps, kings;
casings give way from the old studs.
With slow hands he passes down the frames.

After so many years of bottles and trash,
old fridges, cars like carcasses in the yard,
how can a thing bear changing views?

I reach. I hold the window against the sky,
see through its invisibility.
Like me.

WU

There Are Indications of Intense Depression Forming . . .

When invisibility doesn't work, I walk out
of laundry, longings, talk

as raw as the venison
I am thawing for supper

down to water, and sand soft as dough.
Alewife die-off.

Today the wind pushes the ice north.
Warming trend,

but on the horizon,
waves shaped like pinking shears.

I'd rather have it straight cold
than this false balm

laced with tiny silver corpses
and stinking air.

Given the signals—mist
at Good Harbor, fog at Otter Creek,

I could forecast this storm
if I were blind. I'm not.

What I know on other days
grows from this weather coming on.

The dunes do not fight the wind.
Sand flies where it is told.

I am a fish from its only sea—
with one way to live,

and I took it with both hands
from my black-eyed daddy.

I am the hollow, the empty
bowl that shapes a lake.

D

Keep Clear of Me; I Am Maneuvering with Difficulty

So I have to get drunk
over at Art's

where the boys know Barn
and leave me alone.

I know right away it'll get around
and someone will tell his mama,

but I stay committed
until I'm so gone I can laugh.

One of his poaching buddies says,
Bead, I'll take you home,

but I say, *No.* I say,
Don't touch me anywhere.

He backs off, palms up.
I toss back my Jack

remembering how to keep distance
from men, friends, the past

that still lives. Time I pay
my tab and go.

Just offshore, I spot the mannequin
bobbing inside the green pool

poured down by the coast guard beacon.
After pretending one way and another

for an hour, I know for sure.
It's no fucking doll.

I'm too drunk to swim out
and pull her in,

and too scared to touch her,
let her touch me.

And that's the problem.
No way to get to her

or get away, get past the fact
of that blue-black death

staring me in the face
like a dog trained to kill.

I finally know, I'm not letting her go,
no matter how I'd like to.

I sober up quick,
stagger back to the bar, call 911.

Sirens and flashing lights.
I lay in the sand, thinking hard

about the drift of being drunk,
the way it pushes in and out

as though we are just bodies
without anything to feel,

as though we are dead.
The way she's dead.

Someone, then no one.
If, if, if.

And part of me wants to say—
what's the dif?

And another part sees her eyes,
watered down

to smithereens with what she's seen.
And it's that look

that finally gets to me,
makes me remember how

we are stuck on this stripe
of mud and unemployment

of the heart, always mired
in each other and memory.

I walk all the way home, tell Barn a lie
so I can crawl into this one night

before he knows what I know:
How we run,

man do we run, straight
into the eyes of our secret dead.

PH 2

I Am Steering towards You

I stand outside his mama's house, read
the peeled paint like it could tell me what to do.
I knock soft as not being there.

I've lived here long enough to see
their dead as bad as my own.
Makes me think maybe someone old

and smart from the cold
could hold the ground I stand on,
not let quicksand suck me down

where I'd get buried with the rest
of the wrecks. If one person will
let me speak, someone who's

taught me how, yes, how to clean
croppies and suckers, I might believe
the life he tells me I am living.

Quiet as winter,
just as deadly,
she opens the door.

What Is Your Cargo?

His mama, Belly Ann, grows worms
in her basement, making compost
for the spring peas, early greens.
She asks me down. I watch her,

puttering and content as pansies,
surrounded by moldy stones
and Kalkaska sand
they only got here in Michigan.

There's five trays heaped like dog food.
Smallest been eating the longest;
biggest just got fed. At first she gives
just what it says

in the worm farm brochure:
newspaper, old greens,
vegetable refuse, all that.
But they eat so fast,

and what's left is tiny hashed spirals
so small they're fingers to a fist.
She starts in on real leftovers.
She's into it.

Cereal, white bread, half
a freezer-burned roast,
box cinnamon rolls
from the surplus—

they take it all, curl around,
loop slyly in and out
of each other, eating and casting off,
that's what they call it,

castings, like something molded
from bronze, and just that dark.
I can hear them rustling under
the silence, older than memory.

I kneel with her by the troughs.
I ask, *Will they eat anything?*
She smokes a doobie. *Any damn thing.*
I look at her, maybe first time. *A memory?*

She looks back, eyes like the forked tree,
that kind of divided, then blows out haze.
Nothing eats that, Beadie. We carry it always.
But if it helps you, I'll stay with you.

She touches my hands
when I start to cry.
What, girl? You can tell me.
Or tell the worms.

It's all there. Smarm of greens cooked ugly,
sour laughter we ate like cake,
monsoon for twenty days straight.
Cats trapped in walls.

Moldy okra. Rum at dawn,
dirty finger gouging the jam,
flat of the land, flat of a pan,
flat of the hand gone wrong,

animal heart smoked wet, rotted, force-fed,
mouth hinged open by knuckles,
mouth hinged open by the mouth
of a man.

Your daddy? she asks.
Herons so white they mock your scars.
Giant over your—my—bed.
Again. If. Again. If.

If it was me drilled the holes, he died
dead drunk on a boat sunk in the gator pool.
Moss and loss, murder and worms.
It was me. No ifs.

They say we come from water.
I know better. This is us,
castings of worms,
manure, feces, scat—all just words for shit.

EP

I Have Lost Sight of You

I try hard to do it. I wear
his waders into the part
of the channel that is fast

as a shooting star,
deep as a fault line.
I think to leave my reel

on the shore and let the rod
he gave me for opening day
go adrift. Good-bye enough.

I wade out past logs,
where the drop-off is a tangle
of deadfall old as fear.

All I mean is to lean
into the icy flow, tea colored
and mean with sorrow,

when this old fish, big one,
noses the surface, catches the rush,
pushes toward the weir still a good way up.

She is tired and death is not far off,
and there's no chance she can
leap the grade for higher water.

And still she meets that current
like it meant something to break herself
on that slime-curdled cement.

And I, because I can't read her marks
to call her by her river name,
call her by my own.

YZ

The Words which Follow Are in Plain Language

Instead, I run away.

Then the cursed wonder of it,
waking up in the sun in the cab—
having gotten stuck on some muck track
and busted the timing chain
in my rust-peppered pickup—
walking five grimy miles
back to the highway,
two more to the local tow,
then the phone,
and through all that limping sunlight,
the crows singing their glee club
chorus about what jerks we all are.
And I look up into the trees
thinking to tell them they are
fucking correct
when it comes to me—

I still have it, I still have it,
this uncertain life,
this one plain, stained thing
with some small horizon
still splitting it in two.

Just to feel it
I kick some side-road rocks so hard
I break my steel-toes.
I turn around, head to the only place
that feels like home.

The Code of Signals

These are what I use for meaning:
distresses between vessels,

ciphered glances over a shot of scotch,
cool curve of his arm in sleep;

how I speak when speech is shaped
by weather, groceries, short distances.

I have learned that love makes words
with storm, water, even fists

and the secrets we keep from the world
turn on themselves, become an alphabet

coded with the currents of our days—
a scum line which, when finally read,

spells out,
oh, what the hell is it?—

Sorrow?
Rare, befuddled joy?

about the author

 Anne-Marie Oomen is a poet, playwright, and essayist. Her memoir *Pulling Down the Barn* was a 2005 Michigan Notable Book, and her award-winning poem-script, "Northern Belles," a play based on rural women farmers, has been produced across the Midwest. Oomen is the founding editor of the *Dunes Review* and serves as chair of the Creative Writing Department at Interlochen Arts Academy. She lives near Traverse City, Michigan.

acknowledgments

Earlier versions of the following poems, "KS1 I Have Taken the Line," "OO My Radio Direction Finder Is Inoperative," and "NE You Should Proceed with Great Caution" were published in the *Dunes Review: Literary Journal of Northern Michigan*.

I'd like to thank H. Emerson Blake for his insightful first response on this manuscript, James Cihlar at Milkweed for his patience as I worked through the changes, but most especially Laure-Anne Bosselaar and B. Lee Hope for their unfailing support of the "uncoded woman." I'd also like to thank my colleagues at Interlochen Arts Academy, Mike Delp and Jack Driscoll, who are always with me in this work. My thanks to Sleeping Bear Dunes National Lakeshore volunteers at the Lifesaver's Museum for information about the International Code of Signals. Blessings on the sauna family and my beloved, David Early—without you, pen doesn't touch paper.

More Poetry from Milkweed Editions

Blue Lash
James Armstrong

Turning Over the Earth
Ralph Black

*Urban Nature: Poems
about Wildlife in the City*
Edited by Laure-Anne
Bosselaar

*Astonishing World:
The Selected Poems of
Ángel González 1956–1986*
Translated from the Spanish
by Steven Ford Brown and
Gutierrez Revuelta

*The Phoenix Gone,
The Terrace Empty*
Marilyn Chin

*The Art of Writing:
Lu Chi's* Wen Fu
Translated from the Chinese
by Sam Hamill

Playing the Black Piano
Bill Holm

Good Heart
Deborah Keenan

Furia
Orlando Ricardo Menes

*The Porcelain Apes of
Moses Mendelssohn*
Jean Nordhaus

*Firekeeper:
Selected Poems*
Pattiann Rogers

Some Church
David Romtvedt

*For My Father, Falling Asleep
at Saint Mary's Hospital*
Dennis Sampson

Atlas
Katrina Vandenberg

**To order books or for more information, contact Milkweed at
(800) 520-6455 or visit our Web site (www.milkweed.org).**

MILKWEED ✦ EDITIONS

Founded in 1979, Milkweed Editions is one of the largest independent, nonprofit literary publishers in the United States. Milkweed publishes with the intention of making a humane impact on society, in the belief that literature can transform the human heart and spirit. Within this mission, Milkweed publishes in four areas: fiction, nonfiction, poetry, and children's literature for middle-grade readers.

Join Us

Milkweed depends on the generosity of foundations and individuals like you, in addition to the sales of its books. In an increasingly consolidated and bottom-line-driven publishing world, your support allows us to select and publish books on the basis of their literary quality and the depth of their message. Please visit our Web site (www.milkweed.org) or contact us at (800) 520-6455 to learn more about our donor program.

Interior design and typesetting by Percolator
Typeset in Miller Text, Miller Display, and Aachen
Printed on acid-free Glatfelter paper
by Friesens Corporation

Printed in the USA
CPSIA information can be obtained
at www.ICGtesting.com
JSHW080005150824
68134JS00021B/2296